BROKEN WORDS

By: Monica D. Robinson

Illustrated By
Nafisa Arshad

THIS BOOK BELONGS TO

Dedication

This book is dedicated to my husband Ray and my daughter Quayle.Thank you both for the love and continued support My bonus nephew Nigel was my inspiration for writing this book.

Enjoy!

BROKEN WORDS

Monica D. Robinson

Illustrated by
Nafisa Arshad

Julia woke up excited and nervous. Today is her first day of third grade.

For the last three years, Julia was home schooled.

She is now wondering about making new friends and being accepted.

As Julia's nerves took over, she pulls the covers back over her head no longer excited about her first day of school.

After hearing a light knock on her bedroom door, Julia's mom walked into her room which is beautifully decorated with butterflies and painted yellow which happens to be Julia's favorite color.

Mrs. Bowlan walked into the room with a smile on her face. She sat next to Julia's bed. " Good morning, sweetie. It's time to get ready for your big day.

Julia pulled the covers down and shook her head from side to side trying her best to speak. As Julia tries very hard not to stutter, she replies "I- I- I don't want to g- g- go".

Her words did not come out as she had hoped. Julia's mom looked at her with concern. "Julia, you have been excited all summer. What's wrong"?

With huge crocodile tears in her eyes, Julia looked at her mom's worried face. Julia started stuttering "Th-th-they will laugh at me".

Mrs. Bowlan held back her own tears as she hugged Julia.

Finally letting go, she looked in Julia's face and said, "Julia, they will not laugh at you. I promise."

Letting go of Julia, Mrs. Bowlan stood and said, "Honey, you have to get up and get dressed now. I have breakfast waiting and the bus will be here soon."

As Mrs. Bowlan walked out of the room, Julia pulled herself together. After getting dressed, Julia walked out of her room. As she entered the kitchen, she saw her father sitting at the table. “Good morning sweet heart. Are you ready for your big day”?

With her head hung, Julia began to cry. She struggled to get her words out. Her mother walks over and places her arms around her daughter.

Mr. Bowlan looked at his wife with a concerned look and then back at Julia. Sadly, Julia looked up at her father.

She took a deep breath, hoping her words would not come out broken as they normally would. “I talk different from the o-o-other kids and I’m sc-sc-scared”, she stuttered.

Julia’s father stopped eating, walked over to her, raised her head, and said, “They will not laugh and you will make friends. How about I drop you off at school today?”

Julia jumped up from her chair, ran over to her dad, and hugged him. After breakfast Julia grabbed her bookbag, still unsure about how she will be treated.

Julia and her dad arrived at Viewpoint Elementary School.

Julia's dad grabs her hand and tries to reassure her that everything will be fine.

Julia reaches down to pick up her bookbag. Pulling on the door handle, she exits the car.

Viewpoint Elementary

Julia began to slowly walk into her new school and down the hallway.

She can feel the butterflies in her stomach as she continues to look for her homeroom class.

As she walks into room 517, she's greeted by her teacher Mrs. Greenly.

She welcomed Julia and asked her to have a seat along with the other students.

INFOGRAPHICS

As the children settled down, Mrs. Greenly introduced herself and asked each child to say their name.

It was now Julia's turn to stand. She knew without a doubt she was going to stutter.

Julia stuttered, "My name is Ju-Ju-Julia." When she was done, Julia put head down and waited for the laughter of her classmates, but it never came.

To her surprise, no one laughed. They clapped and welcomed Julia.

After each student introduced themselves, Julia looked up at Mrs. Greenly with a smile on her face.

Mrs. Greenly gave her a quick wink and proceeded with the lesson.

At that moment Julia knew she was going to have a great school year, because being different no longer mattered.

She learned to embrace her BROKEN WORDS for now.

The End

Glossary

Accepted (ac-cept-ed) generally believed or recognized to be valid or correct.

Different (dif-fer-ent) not the same as another or each other.

Embrace (em-brace) accept or support.

Excited (ex-cit-ed) very enthusiastic and eager.

Homeschool (home-school) to teach school subjects to one's children at home.

Proceed (pro-ceed) begin or continue a course of action.

Reassure (re-as-sure) say or do something to move the doubts or fears of someone.

Stutter (stut-ter) to speak with involuntary disruption or blocking of speech.

About The Author

Hello, my name is Monica Robinson. I live in Virginia with my husband, daughter and dog. This is my first children's book and I look forward to writing many more. I have been an educator for over twenty years. I enjoy reading, teaching and spending time with my family. Thank you for your support and I truly hope you enjoy reading this book.

Meet Julia, a nine-year-old student who has been homeschooled by her parents A new school year is about to begin and Julia will enter school for the very first time. Julia is afraid she will not make friends because of the way she speaks. Julia speaks with a stutter. Her words are sometimes broken which stops Julia from forming a complete sentence. Let's take a journey with Julia as she embarks third grade.

Made in the USA
Coppell, TX
05 August 2021

59989121R00017